David Selbourne

THE DAMNED

LONDON
METHUEN & CO LTD
11 NEW FETTER LANE EC4

First published in Great Britain 1971
by Methuen & Co. Ltd.
11 New Fetter Lane, London EC4
Copyright © 1971 by David Selbourne
Printed in Great Britain
by Cox & Wyman Ltd.
London, Fakenham and Reading
SBN 416 64830 4 (Paperback)
SBN 416 64820 7 (Hardback)

THE DAMNED

The Damned is David Selbourne's fourth full-length play to be published. Seven principal characters, all aware, with mirth, pity and anguish, of the ebbing of their various hopes in life, offer each other consolation and despair by turns, in a gaunt and comic dance.

The photograph on the back of the cover is reproduced by courtesy of Western Morning News.

The Damned

CHARACTERS

THOMAS STRONG, doctor
LAWRENCE PRYNNE, actor
JOHN PRYNNE, clerk
JOHN PATRICK ROSS, teacher
ARTHUR BRACKLEY, postman

ROSIE BRACKLEY, housewife
VIRGINIA BRACKLEY, a young girl

ANNIE, CARMEN, JOSE, LOUISA, TERESA, YVONNE: girls
SAMMY, TERRY: youths

An anonymous Irishman
A housekeeper
A black man

A play in fifteen scenes

SCENE ONE

The elderly DOCTOR STRONG *receives a tray of steaming food at his consulting-room desk from a dowdy* HOUSEKEEPER.
His patient, the middle-aged actor, LAWRENCE PRYNNE, *is lying on a couch, half-naked, bashful. He covers his groin with his hand, as the* HOUSEKEEPER *enters, and as she leaves, passing him.*
Throughout the scene, STRONG *eats and drinks, and* PRYNNE *dresses.*
Exit HOUSEKEEPER.

STRONG (*mouth full*).
> Whitening hair?
> Why not?

PRYNNE (*shouting*).
> What do you mean, why not?!
> My moustache has turned grey as well!
> Look, doctor. See!
> I have become a problem to myself!!

STRONG You're all right, my friend.
> You're as right as rain . . . even cancers will be curable in time . . .
> . . . Anyhow . . . sickness . . . is a messenger of God.

> I'm often sick.

PRYNNE You surprise me.

STRONG It draws us away from useless sorrows,
> And confronts us with real ones.
> Sickness would do you good.
> Heh-heh!
> Pain keeps a man lively and wakes him up!

7

Have some beef!
Bleeding raw.

PRYNNE (*putting on a corset*).
I'm going to die.

STRONG We don't die suddenly, friend.
Take it quietly!

PRYNNE No one has a right to die before old age.

STRONG Worry beats down the most robust,
In time.
Beware, friend.
Take the inevitable firmly.
Be . . . dour.

PRYNNE (*pulling up trousers*).
Grief . . . anxiety . . . worry . . . bad dreams . . . my
son . . . sorrow!
I know them all.
I don't want to die!!

STRONG Good, good.
Death is always preceded by a perfect
willingness to die,
So all is well, my friend.
Just make your will, in case,
And consign all to the redeemer.
Have a drink!

PRYNNE (*fastening his flies*).
How do you . . . to tell my son . . . how do you
recognize the approach of death?
Is it . . .

STRONG . . . . Heh-heh!
Tossings to throw off the bedclothes.
That kind of thing.
A drink, sir.

PRYNNE Tell me all you know,
I beg you!
Please!

STRONG The dying turn to the light.

PRYNNE *turns to the light.*

PRYNNE And then . . . what do they see?

STRONG They see only what is near at hand,

(*Whispering.*) And hear only . . . what is spoken in their ears.

A silence.

PRYNNE What?

STRONG (*shouting*).

And hear only what is spoken in their ears!!

Heh-heh!

Oh, heh-heh!

PRYNNE (*picking up his shirt*).

Ah.

STRONG There are always brief warnings, however slight.

Ample time to call your son, my good fellow.

A short tremor of fright, Prynne,

Heh-heh,

Which must mean a great deal to the vigilant, like

yourself, eh?

A silence.

(*Laughing.*) You feel it now?

PRYNNE Don't frighten me!

Don't jest, doctor!

My skin is firm!

Look, see!

My eyes are clear,

The whites white,

The pupils blue,

Hair thick and healthy.

My body's in fine shape still, Dr Strong.

STRONG Splendid, splendid!

Straight trees are felled first, my friend!

Heh-heh!

PRYNNE I want life!!!

STRONG Oh yes, indeed!

9

Excellent, my friend!

PRYNNE (*putting on socks*).

I have no fear, really.

Not at all.

And a son to succeed me. All a man might ask for.

STRONG Feet cold!

PRYNNE (*afraid*).

Pardon?

STRONG Temples sweating.

You asked me.

Nose pointing.

Face pale or . . . black.

Stiff hands.

PRYNNE Uh?

Not at all.

Everything's normal.

STRONG Physician despairing.

PRYNNE (*putting on tie*).

What are you talking about?

STRONG (*drinking, swaying*).

Hands waving, fumbling,

Friends weeping,

Sucking, the first and last action of man.

Oh, I thirst,

He said, on the cross!!

Tremendum est mortis sacramentum!!

PRYNNE Please!

I don't follow!!!

What are you saying?

STRONG Forgive me, my friend.

Dying is easy, Prynne!

What is there to it? Heh-heh!

Only the palls and the candles,

Ceremonies and sermons,

Ministers and doctors,
And a sprinkling of earth.
There is nothing much to it, my friend.

It has its own raptures, even.

We should be frightened of life, not death,
If we were wise.
Because the whore and the buffoon come off best, sir.
Therefore, avoid melancholy, friend,
Act your part bravely,
Grow from fear to love,
And all shall be well,
And all manner of things shall be well.
Heh-heh!

PRYNNE Love?
You mean . . .

STRONG . . . Love of man.
What else?

PRYNNE *backs away.*

PRYNNE Man? You mean . . . ?

STRONG (*drinking*).
Love of man!!

PRYNNE Ah, yes.
I see.

PRYNNE *puts on his tight shoes. He hobbles.*

STRONG (*gently*).
You walk as if you had both feet in one shoe.
Look at you!

PRYNNE Not at all.

I need . . . your pity, doctor.

STRONG The world is made of those who need pity,
And those who refuse it.
One or the other.

I refuse it.

PRYNNE I don't . . . enjoy anything!!

I told you.

I've lost my strength . . . down here.

I can't feel it!

STRONG (*angrily*).

And what would you like best, eh?

What can we offer?!

PRYNNE I'd like a soft delicate life,

When I'm afraid.

To be a loving father, a gentle lover.

I'm sorry, doctor.

I have a boy's mind.

And body, doctor.

I'm not . . . made right, am I?

I . . . used to be a good actor.

Tell me!

I only want health, doctor.

STRONG You have it, you have it, brother Prynne!

Now, leave me, there's a good fellow.

The quick and the dead cry out!

PRYNNE What is art or religion, I always say,

To a man with an ache in his privates?

Eh, doctor! Isn't that so?

O, have I lost my health and youth?

STRONG *seizes hold of* PRYNNE.

Don't, doctor!

STRONG To and fro,

To and fro, eh, full of nervous thought,

Like a duck in a pool!

PRYNNE Don't shake me, don't shake me!

STRONG O, drink to me only!

PRYNNE Forgive me. Be my friend.

STRONG (*pouring a drink*).

My tongue cleaves to the roof of my mouth.

Good health,
And long life, sir!
Stand up and storm the gates of heaven,
Prynne!!

PRYNNE You're mocking me.
You should be ashamed,
A man in your station.

STRONG Mercy! Mercy!

PRYNNE You're a good talker,
But a bad listener, doctor.

STRONG No needle is sharp at both ends.
Have a drink, sir!!

PRYNNE No, sir.
I don't.
The anarchy of drink, I call it.
A poor example. The itch of gluttony, also.

STRONG You don't.
I see.
Enjoy your misery then, friend. Life is whatever
you want.
Death can do no more than kill you.

PRYNNE You have bemused me.

STRONG A man with a grievance is always happy.

PRYNNE You avoid the issue,
Lying and joking.
You conceal the truth.
You have no discipline, doctor.
You are always mocking.
Where's my prescription?

STRONG (*gathering up boxes of pills*).
A sweet morsel under your tongue,
Or gravel in the mouth,
It's up to you,
And these up your back passage.
Heh-heh.

13

PRYNNE How you disappoint me!

STRONG (*arm around* PRYNNE).

Medicine only cures the man who is fated to get well, sir.

PRYNNE Let me go now.

STRONG The little bird lives in a mighty forest.

PRYNNE Yes, doctor.

STRONG He occupies only a single twig.

PRYNNE That's it, doctor.

Of course he does.

STRONG (*sniffing*).

Even the best plastic flowers have no smell.

PRYNNE Let me go now.

A clock strikes.

STRONG Minutes strike on, counted by angels.

Bow to me, Prynne!

Bow low, eh?

If you bow at all, bow low!

How long is it since you've worked,

Eh, Prynne?

How long resting?

Tell me again for the pleasure of hearing you speak!

PRYNNE Seven years . . .

STRONG *convulsed with laughter.*

. . . Seven years,

Saddened and darkened by pains and illnesses.

STRONG And a deceased shrewish wife, and an erring son?

PRYNNE I have racked my brains day and night,

To find out the meaning of it all . . .

STRONG . . . Splendid, splendid!

To be virtuous a man must be able to suffer,

Eh, Prynne, eh my good fellow? . . .

PRYNNE . . . If I could get hold of that,

I'd be on the high road to health again.

Truth lies in a nutshell, doctor . . .

STRONG . . . . For those who have nutcrackers, my friend,
Eh?

PRYNNE Yes, doctor, that's so true.
But sickness mars and embitters my life . . .

STRONG . . . True, true! Go on, go on!

PRYNNE Truth fades away from my sick vision!
But, one day,
Illness shall be expelled from earth!!
The stage teaches us that triumph is a matter only
of willpower . . .

STRONG (*speech slurred*).
. . . Take your life in your teeth,
That's it, my friend.
Stand up and storm the gates of heaven, Prynne!
Adam and Eve . . .
. . . In the Garden of Eden . . .
Ate vegetables and fruit.
That was their meat.

PRYNNE The root of the matter is found in me.
I shall be strong once more!

STRONG I must have another drink.

PRYNNE I'll go now.

STRONG Don't play with the spoon, Prynne,
Before you take the dose, eh?
Heh-heh.
That's it.

PRYNNE (*limping*).
I'll be back.
Exit PRYNNE.

STRONG (*drinking*).
The host is happy,
When the guest is gone.

SCENE TWO

A classroom.

On a platform, ROSS, *a torpid and rotund thirty-year-old teacher, with a blackboard headed 'Civics' and inscribed with illegible phrases, behind him. A small class of youths and girls, which includes the sixteen-year-old* VIRGINIA BRACKLEY, *a leather-jacketed youth* TERRY, *a black youth* SAMMY, *a bespectacled earnest girl* ANNIE, *who takes notes, and* LOUISA, *holding hands with* TERRY.

As ROSS *speaks, with droning voice, restlessness; and whenever he turns to write on the board,* LOUISA *and* TERRY *kiss and grapple, with increasing ardour.*

ROSS . . . evaluate the meaning of the present trend,
And point up certain specific factors in our culture.
The central fact is the inhibition of intra-familial communication.
Groans. ROSS *writes 'intra-familial communication'.*
The life pattern, the life plan,
The total life situation,
Remains unformed.
This is not to deny that adolescence is not the time of necessary rebellion,
Of the search for what comes truly from within,
And which, therefore, seems real,
And of the formation of what we may call identity . . .
ROSS *writes 'identity'.*
. . . the internal gyroscope of conscience.
Any questions?
Yes?

TERRY What exactly do you mean?

I mean, what do you mean – adolescence and all that?

Laughter.

ROSS Self-consciousness, without self-awareness,
First of all.

VIRGINIA I don't understand really. I mean . . . sort of . . .

ROSS . . . Uncertainty, Virginia, dissatisfaction, self-doubt,
A lack of will,
Indolence and lethargy, maybe.

TERRY Are you saying that we're . . .

ROSS . . . Maturity alone brings . . .

LOUISA . . . What's maturity then, go on, clever?

ROSS (*gazing off*).
The ability to postpone gratification,
To undergo present discomfort,
In order to gain greater pleasure, at some other time.
Oh, I don't know.
Identity formation . . . values . . . conscience perhaps,
That sort of thing.

TERRY Could you write it all down, sir?

LOUISA We don't quite follow, really, honestly!

VIRGINIA Louisa!

Laughter.

ROSS Certainly, Louisa . . .

ROSS *begins to write,* LOUISA *and* TERRY *kissing.*
ROSS *turns round, and watches, expressionless.*
Laughter.

. . . Some, without these things . . .
. . . May feel themselves . . .

Laughter.

. . . May feel themselves becoming steadily more bored and lethargic,
Retreating deeper into introspection,

Unable to marshal sufficient will and strength,
To overcome the descent towards what's known as
inertia . . .

VIRGINIA . . . Are you bored as well, sir?
Forgive me for asking.

ROSS . . . A descent so rapid and without explanation,
That one fears, at any moment,
Suicidal impulses might arise,
And be acted upon.

LOUISA *and* TERRY *openly grappling.*

VIRGINIA It's not true, sir, really,
Honestly, it isn't,
You've got to believe in something or somebody,
that's all!

ROSS Few are capable of that leap of faith.

TERRY (*kissing* LOUISA).
Everyone's got an aim, haven't they?

ROSS Pardon?
Mutterings.
Silence!
Jeering.

ANNIE What about religion then?

ROSS (*angrily*).
The sick make a religion of health,
The chaste a religion of love, and so forth,
What you will.
Merely the tenor of the times and men, no more . . .

ANNIE . . . Sir, sir, let me speak . . .
Christ said . . . I feel . . . I mean, god . . .
Groans.

ROSS . . . This is false feeling . . .

TERRY (*stroking* LOUISA).
. . . And this is real, baby!

ROSS . . . An assertion that cannot be tested . . .

ANNIE . . . It's common sense, isn't it?

ROSS Sense is not very common, I'm afraid.

TERRY Ooh, sarcky!

Laughter.

ANNIE You're wrong, you're wrong!

ROSS Right and wrong are two sides of the same coin.

ANNIE I've got a right to say what I think.

ROSS Only if I agree.

So you have no right.

I am your teacher.

Jeering.

SAMMY (*standing up*).

You bloody tyrant!

We've had enough, haven't we, eh?

You can't do this to us, blinding on and on,

We're human, ain't we?

We got a voice!

Answer!

ALL Answer, answer!!

ROSS You are, boys and girls,

What I call, a chaos, merely.

ANNIE You're evil!

You're the devil!

ROSS The tendency, Annie,

To classify men as good or evil, god or devil,

Tall or short,

Black or white, my friend,

Valiant or coward,

Is a game of words,

And indicates nothing of their nature.

The class screams, in unison, with hatred.

SAMMY We'll kill you!

VIRGINIA *tries to stop* SAMMY *grabbing* ROSS; *a scuffle.* ROSS *stumbles.*

VIRGINIA Please, sir! Don't, Sammy!

We can't take it any more, we can't!

A silence.

ANY VOICE He wants locking up.

ROSS The gaoler lives in the prison too.

ANY VOICE The government can make you.

ROSS What is the government?

A body of men.

I am a man.

I am part of the government too.

ANY VOICE They can lock you up.

ROSS Then they have failed.

They have not made me perform anything,

Against my will,

So I remain free.

And the gaoler lives in the prison too.

All groan.

ANY VOICE Forget him. Let's get out!

SAMMY Come on, cats!

(*Jigging.*) Let's go dancing!

ANY VOICE We'll report you, we will.

ANY VOICE You've had it then, sir.

ANY VOICE He's having us on.

He's putting on an act.

Let's leave him.

SAMMY C'mon, kids,

Let's beat it!

VIRGINIA I don't think we should.

There'll be terrible trouble.

ROSS *laughs.*

Teaching can be very valuable sometimes.

Jeers.

ROSS Value consists only in what men decide is valuable.

Nothing is truly valuable, my dear.

You are free to go.

ANY VOICE What if we fight you?

ROSS Men must co-operate to fight.

Therefore you cannot fight me.

ANNIE (*screaming*).

I must be dreaming!!

Please!

I'm screaming!!

She seizes SAMMY, *kissing and fondling him in a rage, crying.*

I must be dreaming!!

ROSS We are awake,

As long as we know we are dreaming.

When we are awake, we forget we are awake,

And so are dreaming.

SAMMY You're a slave!

ROSS It depends on where you stand.

From where I stand, Sammy,

Looking down on you,

It is wholly different.

It is you who are slaves, entirely.

A bell rings.

You may go now.

SCENE THREE

A park bench in the sun. The roar of traffic can be heard in the distance. Bird-song. PRYNNE *immaculately dressed, with gold-topped cane and button-hole, and holding himself stiffly upright, sits taking the sun, eyes closed. He now has a black toupée, and black moustache. At the other end of the bench,* JOHN PRYNNE, *his son, in his mid-twenties, in crumpled dark suit, dishevelled and weary, with a briefcase and rolled up newspaper.* JOHN PRYNNE *eyes* PRYNNE *during a long silence, the latter oblivious.*

JOHN PRYNNE Got a light, sir?

A silence. JOHN PRYNNE *registers defeat; unfolds his newspaper. While he reads, a black man passes, unnoticed.* PRYNNE *opens his eyes, blinks, looks anxiously at his fob-watch, and takes a pill.*

Have you got a light?

So sorry to disturb you, father.

PRYNNE Indeed I have.

I am radiant again with the fire of the sun,

And you shall feed your dead torch,

At my eternal flame!

PRYNNE *produces a gold lighter and deftly flicks a flame.* JOHN PRYNNE *clumsily blows it out.*

Suck, don't blow, son!

Heh-heh!

JOHN PRYNNE *puffs angrily.* PRYNNE *drinks fastidiously from a medicine bottle.*

Illness shall be expelled from the earth.

The root of the matter is found in me.

The black man passes by.

JOHN PRYNNE A lovely English garden, this,

Isn't it, father?

PRYNNE Rus in urbe, son, rus in urbe.

JOHN PRYNNE Russian . . . ? Where?

PRYNNE . . . A rural spot in the teeming town.

JOHN PRYNNE Beautiful.

Can't beat it.

Not like it used to be, though,

I don't expect.

You'd know, sir.

PRYNNE Fresh flowers of the field.

Aah, the open air!

The sight of all this sweetness.

I feel young again, my son.

22

JOHN PRYNNE You look splendid, sir.
A proud figure of a man,
If I may say so.

PRYNNE Do not be misled by appearance, my boy.
It is within that the canker grows,
In the blown rose,
And the addled brain.
The black man passes by.

JOHN PRYNNE There's a cancer in our midst,
Eh, is that it, father?

PRYNNE Even cancers are curable if caught in time.
That is my information.
(*Taking a pill.*) Don't let worry beat you down.
See your doctor soon.
Allay your fears.

Take your life in your teeth, son.
My job is done.
The root of the matter is found in you.

JOHN PRYNNE You mean . . . you mean . . .
We must all have pride?

PRYNNE Illness shall be expelled from earth.
It is a matter of the will alone.

JOHN PRYNNE And strength, eh, father?
Strength and pride and power?

PRYNNE I have much to be thankful for.
Despite your bad behaviour,
My body's in fine shape still.
Only a few private troubles remaining,
That you could never understand.
I won't bother you with them.
They're not for you.

Crucify your lusts, son.
We are all servants of the groin.

23

JOHN PRYNNE You've got it there, dad.
Nothing to beat it.
That's the life.
Love them and leave them,
I always say.

PRYNNE The sigh, the groan, of the act of love,
Beckon all men, young and old.

JOHN PRYNNE They do, they do.
Hit the bally nail on the head there, father!

PRYNNE (*seizing his son*).
Resist!
Resist!!
We have the appetites of beasts!!
Enter VIRGINIA *demurely. She sits down between
them.*

VIRGINIA You ought to be ashamed,
Grown men like you,
Carrying on like that,
It isn't . . . dignified.

You might look worried,
Carrying on like that in public,
All dressed up too.

PRYNNE I have no worries.

VIRGINIA You liar!
We've all got worries.
It's only human, isn't it?

PRYNNE When you get to my age,
You have no worries.

VIRGINIA Your age?!
Who are you then? Methuselah?
She giggles.

PRYNNE I take the inevitable firmly, my dear.

VIRGINIA Ooh-lah-de da!
I had no idea.

What's that stick you've got, then?
Is it gold?

JOHN PRYNNE Don't upset him.

PRYNNE A gold topped cane, my child.
A poseur's prop.
Heh-heh.

VIRGINIA Is it gold, then?

PRYNNE It is, my dear.

VIRGINIA Are you very rich?

PRYNNE I have what I need,
I need what I have.

VIRGINIA Isn't he a skinflint?

JOHN PRYNNE Please!

VIRGINIA Are you a dirty old man?

JOHN PRYNNE I'm a dirty young man!
Huh-huh!

VIRGINIA Oo, you disgusting!
I'm not stopping here.
It isn't safe.

PRYNNE (taking her hand).
How old are you, my child?

VIRGINIA Sixteen, seventeen nearly.

PRYNNE Aaah!
Sweet careless rapture of youth!
Green little girl!
Oh, would that I were young again,
As I used to be at twenty-one.

VIRGINIA You're not so old.

PRYNNE I'm a sick man, my dear.
No one knows.

VIRGINIA You look all right, really.
Your hair's a bit peculiar,
More like a wig to look at,
But you look distinguished, honestly.
Anyway, my teacher . . . I'm at the tech . . .

Says there's no difference between anything, really.
I suppose it's all in the mind is what he means.
PRYNNE My body's in fine outward shape still.

My flesh is firm,
My eye is clear.
VIRGINIA Go on with you!
Who's your friend?
PRYNNE I want life!
I want life!!
VIRGINIA Get off me.
You're bruising my arm! Really!
PRYNNE I'm alive with true life now.
My life will be wholly filled by you.
VIRGINIA I'll call the police, I will.
Get off! Please!
Who's your friend, then?
PRYNNE *takes a pill.*
JOHN PRYNNE My name is John Prynne.
Pleased to meet you . . .
VIRGINIA (*shaking hands*).
. . . I'm sure.
PRYNNE Let us take a stroll together.
Through the verdant woods, my dear.
JOHN PRYNNE Don't take liberties with the kid, dad,
She's only young.
VIRGINIA Kid?
Eh, grandpa?
What are you then, eh?

You've got acne, Mr Prynne.
And dandruff.

He might be a bit of a nut,
At least he's sort of freshened up and lively,

That's appealing really, in a way,
Well, it is,
To me.

PRYNNE My life will be wholly filled by you!

VIRGINIA Mine won't be filled by you, mister!

JOHN PRYNNE It's a disgrace!
Talking to her in that shameful manner, in front of
me,
Mauling this sweet girl,
This . . . this flower,
This . . . this English rose,
In an English garden.
It isn't right.
It just isn't right, that's all.

PRYNNE Forgive him, my child, his gallantry,
At my request.
No . . . youth can understand an old man's vision of
purest love.

VIRGINIA I don't understand it, would you believe it,
We were only talking,
It's all in fun, isn't it?

PRYNNE The sight of you makes him hot, my dear.
The fire burns below.

VIRGINIA I was just sitting here in the sunshine,
Sort of escaping,
Passing the time,
Wasn't I?

PRYNNE Only the power of the will beats licence down,
And makes men strong, son.
PRYNNE, *reaching across* VIRGINIA, *taps* JOHN
PRYNNE *on the arm. Son lashes father away.*

VIRGINIA What's the matter with you two?
I haven't done anything,
I was only sitting here,
Minding my own business,

What's wrong with that?

Actually,
I came out . . . to get my legs brown for the holidays.
See!
My . . . boy friend likes them brown,
He's a very sexy one, really,
You ought to see him,
We're going to the Riviera, actually,
Anyhow, I'll be off now,
So nice to have met you,
Bye-bye for now, then,
Shake hands, and make it up,
No hard feelings,
Just for me, eh?
Exit VIRGINIA. *A silence. Birdsong.*

JOHN PRYNNE How disgusting, father!
She was so young and gentle!

PRYNNE She had nothing to fear from me, son.
A silence. PRYNNE *takes a pill.*
I mean no harm!

SCENE FOUR

A strip show, in seedy mid-turn.
Music on a scratching record, multi-coloured moving spots.
A distant sound of traffic.
Sequins, ostrich feathers, a smell of cheap scent, bumps and grinds, CARMEN *stripping.*
Dimly visible, an audience of two men, separately seated, and one man standing.

Seated, JOHN PRYNNE *and* ROSS. *Standing, behind them, in shabby raincoat, and muffler, picking his nose, an anonymous* IRISHMAN.

IRISHMAN Holy stocking-tops! Let me see you, darling!
Bejabbers, see the bursting boobies on her!
O delicious, delightful, delectable, de-lovely Yvonne!
This could be the big one.

This could bust the charts, boy!
This chick'll go places.
Give us more, me darling doll,
Give us more, Kathleen.
Where are we?
Wassername?

JOHN PRYNNE Senorita Carmen, all the way from sunny Spain.

IRISHMAN Get that!
Bejabbers!
To-re-ador, to-re-ador,
To-re-ador, to-re-ador,
To-o-o-re-a-dor, toreador,
To-o-o . . .

CARMEN . . . Waddya bloody think yer doing?

JOHN PRYNNE Hoh-hoh! Well done there.

IRISHMAN Be god, who are you meaning, then?

CARMEN You, mate!

IRISHMAN O, Senorita Carmen.
And you truly coming all the way from darling Spanish Spain,
Talking like that to a poor fella like me,
Bejabbers.

CARMEN You want bouncin', pal?
Eh?

IRISHMAN Bejabbers.

29

CARMEN Are you gonna sit down, and suck yer bleedin'
thumbs?

Get yer hands out of yer bleeding pockets,
You dirty git!

IRISHMAN Be god.

CARMEN Get the bleeder out!

The IRISHMAN *is picked up and thrown out.*

CARMEN *continues, stripping to nudity.* JOHN
PRYNNE *applauds. Interlude music. Arguing voices
behind curtain. Laughter.*

RECORDED ANNOUNCEMENT (*in honeyed, broken English*).

'And now gentlemen, a short intermission. Our
show will continue in ten minutes . . . ten minutes,
with more of our lovelies for your delight. Thank
you.'

JOHN PRYNNE Hot stuff, what?

Got a light, sir?

ROSS I don't smoke.

JOHN PRYNNE What were you saying?

ROSS I wasn't.

JOHN PRYNNE (*lighting cigarette*).

What's your taste, sir?

What sort of thing do you go for?

ROSS Whatever comes along.

JOHN PRYNNE No preferences, not choosy, eh?

Ha-ha!

Well that's up to you, of course.

Give me an English rose, peaches and cream,

Or an Irish maid.

O yes.

What's your line, as a matter of fact?

Forgive me asking.

Business?

Sorry, sorry!
That's me all over.
Talking to everyone.
Irrepressible they call me!
You can't beat it, can you?

I'm in the import-export business.
Africa, Scandinavia, mainly.
Buying and selling, you know.
Bleed the blacks,
And soak the Swedes.
Huh-huh.
Of course, I'm only a small cog in a large machine.
Public school gone wrong, what!
Drop out, throw out, whatever you like.
Stuffed the housemaster's daughter.
Heh-heh.
Good girl, only fourteen.
Of course, she wanted to follow me up to town.
Not bally likely, no sir.
Free and easy.
Love them and leave them.
Eh? Hoh, hoh!

You've got to be cruel to be kind.
That's what I say.
Well you have, haven't you?
Of course, I know where to draw the line.
You just have to, don't you?
I know exactly how far to go.

When to take precautions, when to withdraw.

You'll think me very much of a muchness, I
suppose.

And you'd be darned right, you really would.
You'd hit the nail smack on the bally head
there.
You've certainly got insight, sir.

Lots of yids in this racket.
Dirty bastards, exploiting our people.
Ever have any dealings with them, sir, by any
chance?
Of course you'd probably know, without my saying.
The chosen race, what?
Some choice, some race, eh?

Jewry has a firm grip on our national affairs.
You know that, sir.
The Jewish microbe multiplies in strength,
More rapidly than any known bacillus.
I hardly have to mention it to a man like you.
You'll understand, sir.
We believe it has spread too far to handle.
What we say is, it's all very well to pick their brains,
Unfortunately superior to most of our people's,
Barring present company of course, sir.
But they burrow, burrow, burrow,
Emerging in triumph in posts of power,
Which should be the heritage of our people.
You'd understand, sir,
Without my saying.

Perhaps you'd like to read this, sir . . .
JOHN PRYNNE *thrusts a leaflet at* ROSS.
Music fades.

RECORDED
ANNOUNCEMENT 'And now, gentlemen, continuing our show,
We proudly present to you the one and only,

the delicious, delightful, delectable, de-lovely,
Yvonne!'

Enter, YVONNE, *who strips. The action is carried on
around a tombstone, marked* 'R.I.P.', *on which she
drapes her clothes. The music is a medley of sombre
Tchaikovsky symphonic, and pop. The strip ends.*
JOHN PRYNNE *applauds briefly, and seizes* ROSS.
Music softly.

JOHN PRYNNE Come on!

What do you think?

Out with it!

ROSS I don't.

JOHN PRYNNE You don't agree?

Eh?

ROSS I don't think, friend.

It bores me.

JOHN PRYNNE What do you believe?

Eh?!

Let's have it!

ROSS I have no beliefs.

JOHN PRYNNE Come off it, sir.

You're a yid yourself, aren't you, eh?

A Jew?

ROSS Not as far as I know.

JOHN PRYNNE Ah-ha!

Here's one, friends!

Shamming boredom. Rabbis' alibis, we call them.

That's not a new one,

My word, no.

What's your name?

ROSS Let go.

Don't touch me!

JOHN PRYNNE I'm sorry, sir.

There's only us here.

What's your name?

33

No need for shyness.

ROSS Ross.

JOHN PRYNNE Ross, Ross.

Ye-es!

Rose?

ROSS Ross.

JOHN PRYNNE Cyril? Maurice?

ROSS John Patrick.

JOHN PRYNNE I'll give you the benefit of the doubt, friend.

Many wouldn't.

Anyhow, I think we understand each other,

Don't we?

ROSS I have no beliefs.

I told you.

RECORDED
ANNOUNCEMENT 'In a few moments, gentlemen, we proudly present
to you the delightful, delectable, dusky, Jose.'

Music, softly.

JOHN PRYNNE Another nig.

I'll be moving, friend.

Call them women, huh, nice tits, that's all,

That doesn't make a woman.

And you're a bloody yid in hiding, aren't you, eh?

I can see it in your eye, sir.

Huh-huh!

ROSS (*shouting*).

I have no beliefs!

I have neither wish nor will!!

I am sunk in a life-long stasis!

You wouldn't understand, boy.

Enter JOSE.

JOHN PRYNNE I understand, sir.

Don't call me boy, sir!

ROSS I'm a sloth,

I'm a sloth!!

34

JOHN PRYNNE O.K., sir.

You pass.

Yids don't generally talk like that, sir.

I'm off.

Can't stand the stink of nigger sweat,

You understand me.

ROSS My body is wearied with sleep.

JOHN PRYNNE (*giving leaflets to* ROSS).

Give these to all your friends, sir.

You're a fine decent fellow.

Send us a sub, sir.

The address is on the leaflet.

Be on your guard, sir.

Exit JOHN PRYNNE.

ROSS The mould grows on my coat.

I can't keep awake.

I fall into a sleep,

Akin to death.

ROSS *closes his eyes.*

The music roars on.

SCENE FIVE

In the presence of the blue flickering screen, the BRACKLEY *family together. Only the top of his head and his elbows visible in a high-backed armchair,* ARTHUR BRACKLEY; *in a similar chair, in profile,* ROSIE, *cowed; away from them, facing the audience,* VIRGINIA.

VIRGINIA So . . . so *galante* he is,

So longing really.

35

So polite and speaks so nice and all,
O mum,
I am a lucky person.

But I'm so cruel!
ROSIE Don't fret, my love.
ARTHUR Shurrup,
You pair of bleeders!
I can't hear a bloody word, can I?
VIRGINIA I was so cruel.
I told him, that day we first met,
His dandruff disturbed me.
I could . . . bite my tongue off,
It was so cruel.
ROSIE How could you!
As long as he's got a smile in his heart,
'Ginia,
He'll be a nice person.
VIRGINIA It's worry, mother.
Worrying about this and that,
Import-export, export-import,
Dictating letters himself to all over,
He's got an exceedingly good job, dad.
ARTHUR Bleeding clerk more like, pen-pusher,
Wait till he gets here,
I'll show him,
No one's going to pull the wool on me, girl,
That's final!
ROSIE Arthur!
ARTHUR When I get my hands on the bleeder,
We'll have a snowstorm of dandruff,
A bloody blizzard,
Flying all over!
Heh-heh!
VIRGINIA You'd have dandruff, if you were him, baldy,

All that responsibility and anxiety.

ROSIE Shush! Don't be so provoking!

VIRGINIA Sorry, mother.

Waiting in the park for weeks,
So patient,
Sitting on that bench he was,
Till he should find me,
And one day I came by chance,
And saw him sat there,
Holding some freesias . . .

ARTHUR . . . O my gawd, for god's sake . . .

VIRGINIA . . . Buying them every day,
To greet me when he saw me . . .

ROSIE It's like a real romance, Arthur!
He's found his love and beauty,
Hasn't he, my dear?!
Arthur, look at your charming daughter!

ARTHUR What's he wanna buy her flowers for, eh?
I ask you!
What's he want off of her then, eh?

ROSIE Oh, Arthur!

VIRGINIA . . . And fighting another man for me.
There was this fancy fellow, mother,
An important person, really,
Bow-tie and sprats, like going racing,
Sitting there with this solid gold stick,
God knows who he was,
Trying to chat me up!
She laughs.

ARTHUR It's bloody disgraceful, mother,
Picking up men like that,
At her age!

VIRGINIA He tried to get off with me, he did,
Promising me this and that,

37

        Presents and fancies,

        Asking me to go with him in the radiant
        woods!

ROSIE O, my sweet, my little dove,

        You're my daughter, aren't you?

        She's so romantic. Don't let them hurt you!

ARTHUR And what about bloody Lord Goldstick-in-
        Waiting!

VIRGINIA Mother!

        Listen!

        Anyway, he says . . .

ARTHUR . . . Who says . . . ?

ROSIE He says, Arthur . . .

VIRGINIA John . . . says . . .

ROSIE John Prynne, that's the young lad's name,
        dad . . .

VIRGINIA He's an executive, mother!

ARTHUR All right, let's get the bleeding saga over . . .

VIRGINIA Would I go into the woods?

        I will not, say I,

        I've got a boy friend already,

        I had to tell a lie, really!

        Didn't I, mother, a white one?

ROSIE All's fair in love and war, my love.

        There's only one thing these men are after,

        And you hold on to it.

        Keep your legs crossed, my mum told me.

        ARTHUR *guffaws*.

        Watch your P's and Q's, you know,

        In a manner of speaking.

        Go on, don't mind him.

ARTHUR He's a bloody fast worker,

        This John git, ain't he?

VIRGINIA Are you deaf, dad?

        It breaks my heart talking to you.

It was the other fellow, dad.
Why don't you listen?

ARTHUR (*roaring*).
Why don't I listen?!!!

ROSIE Arthur!

ARTHUR I'll tell you why not, kiddo!
I've been at work all bleeding day,
And I've got enough on my bloody china,
Without all this bloody glob you're serving up!

VIRGINIA O, dad!
(*Head in hands.*) How tragic!

ROSIE Go on, my love,
You tell your Rosie.

VIRGINIA Up he jumps, that's Johnny,
Quick as that,
And says, I'll punch you one if you don't keep
quiet!
You take your hands off her.

ARTHUR And what was he doing then?
Having a damn good feel?
Was he after the meat in the middle of your
sandwich, eh?

VIRGINIA He was holding my very own and precious arm,
As a matter of actuality, father,
And don't be so . . . common!

ARTHUR Whoo-hoo, eh, listen to her,
Little Miss-Bleeding-Distressed-Gentlefolk!

ROSIE They held hands, Arthur,
Like we used to, in Kew Gardens,
Once upon a time, you remember.

ARTHUR And that's bloody ancient history,
I'm telling you, my girl.
A fine sight you look,
Talking all this soft stuff.

ROSIE Don't take liberties with the girl,

That's all I'm asking.

VIRGINIA My John says,

She's so sweet and young,

I have a vision, John said.

ARTHUR Oh, my gawd!

I can't take it any bloody more!

Mercy! Mercy!!

ROSIE Go on, darling!

VIRGINIA A vision of purest love.

This flower, he said,

This English rose.

ARTHUR I thought they were bloody freesias,

Right,

That does it!!

He turns up the TV set's volume to a roar.

VIRGINIA (*shouting*).

He says, he says,

You're a flower, my love, my little love,

(*Crying.*) You're a beautiful English rose!

ARTHUR Yeh!

The bloody git!

And did he want to pluck you?

ROSIE Arthur!!

O how could you!

I'll get that bleeding TV turned off,

If it's the last bleeding thing I do.

ARTHUR *and* ROSIE *struggle. The TV is turned off.*

A silence.

You aren't nice to know, Arthur Brackley.

Virginia's growing up,

She's a person,

I don't know what we're coming to in here,

We've got no lives to speak of,

All this language,

We must grow to love one another,

It's a shame, you wicked creature,
To talk like that.

I shall tell the doctor.

VIRGINIA He doesn't know any better, mother,
He's suffering from what's known as inertia,
He's just . . . uncouth!

ARTHUR Did you say uncouth?

VIRGINIA Yes, I did.

ROSIE *whimpers.*

ARTHUR I see.

Do I have to wash my bleeding ears out,
Or did I hear you say uncouth?

ROSIE (*to* VIRGINIA).
Don't, love.

VIRGINIA You might have.

ARTHUR I see.

Who are you?

VIRGINIA Virginia Brackley.

ROSIE Don't go on, you two!

ARTHUR Aged?

VIRGINIA Seventeen.

ROSIE She's seventeen now, dad.

ARTHUR Daughter of . . . ?

VIRGINIA Arthur Brackley, father.

ARTHUR Aged?

VIRGINIA Fifty-nine.

ROSIE *whimpers.*

ARTHUR And who is Arthur Brackley?

VIRGINIA He works for the G.P.O.

ARTHUR I see.

And what is the G.P.O.?

VIRGINIA General Post Office, father.

ARTHUR And what is his employment?

VIRGINIA Postman, dad.

       Don't go on.

ARTHUR And how many postmen does the General Post Office have in its employ?

VIRGINIA Ninety-nine thousand five hundred, dad.

ARTHUR And what is their task?

VIRGINIA Delivering letters and that to people's houses; and parcels.

ARTHUR And what is their remuneration?

VIRGINIA Eighteen pounds, eight shillings a week, maximum, dad, before deductions.

ARTHUR And how long has Arthur Brackley been in their employ,

       Man and boy?

VIRGINIA Thirty-one years, dad.

ARTHUR And what time of a morning does he get up?

VIRGINIA About four-fifteen, dad.

ARTHUR And am I entitled to speak my bleeding mind on the G.P.O.?

VIRGINIA Yes, dad.

ARTHUR And am I entitled to use any bleeding language I like about it?

ROSIE No, Arthur.

VIRGINIA Yes, dad.

ARTHUR And will that bleeding language get into my bleeding general parlance?

VIRGINIA Yes, dad.

ARTHUR And will it sound uncouth?

VIRGINIA Yes, dad.

ARTHUR And are you bleeding surprised?

VIRGINIA No, dad.

    (*Softly.*) You're a slave, dad, entirely.

ARTHUR Right then!

       That's settled!

I think we know what's what,
I'll have no more of your lip,
Bleeding executive or no executive,
Bleeding freesias, or bleeding roses,
I'm Arthur Brackley of the G.P.O., and that's
that!!!

Exit ARTHUR BRACKLEY.

A silence. A bell rings.

VIRGINIA It's him, mum. I feel so happy, I don't know
myself.

ROSIE We're all bodies, my love, aren't we,
But don't let him, 'Ginia,
Will you,
Not just yet?

The bell rings again. ROSIE *kisses* VIRGINIA *on the
cheek.*

Exit ROSIE, *one way, and* VIRGINIA, *another.*

VIRGINIA *re-enters with* JOHN PRYNNE.

JOHN PRYNNE How charming!
Parents not about?
What a shame!
Hoping to meet them.

VIRGINIA Mother's left us to . . . our own devices, you know.
My dad's . . . upset.

JOHN PRYNNE I see.

VIRGINIA I'm glad you came, John.
I thought you wouldn't come, John. Really.

JOHN PRYNNE I said I'd come, didn't I?
I don't break my word, you know,
Don't start thinking that!

VIRGINIA I wouldn't think that . . . I mean . . .

JOHN PRYNNE . . . If I say I'll come, I come. It's all quite simple.

VIRGINIA Didn't you want to?

JOHN PRYNNE I wanted to come, yes, yes.
Talk to your old man, and so on.

You know.
See you again, of course.
I like meeting people.
Keep off politics and religion,
That's what I say though.
No good falling out with friends, eh,
Is there?
No good at all.

VIRGINIA John . . .

JOHN PRYNNE . . . Hm?

VIRGINIA Johnny . . .

JOHN PRYNNE Call me John,
I don't like it . . .

VIRGINIA . . . I dreamt about you the other night, I did.

JOHN PRYNNE What do you want to do a thing like that for, eh,
Heh-heh?!

VIRGINIA I dreamt you gave me some freesias.
They're my favourites, really.
Flowers.

JOHN PRYNNE I'm not great at that kind of thing,
I'm afraid.
Never given flowers to a woman.
Still there's always a first time, I suppose.

VIRGINIA They're quite cheap, really.

JOHN PRYNNE Oh, it's not the money side, don't get me wrong.
That's no trouble, no trouble at all.
I wouldn't think of a thing like that!
They're just not . . . well . . . not my cup of tea.

VIRGINIA Would you . . . like a cup of tea?

JOHN PRYNNE Very acceptable. Thanks. I will.

VIRGINIA I thought you were so . . . polite and nice and
charming . . .

JOHN PRYNNE . . . I said thanks, didn't I?!!
What was wrong with that?
I don't quite understand you.

44

VIRGINIA You couldn't care for me.

JOHN PRYNNE Please! Come on!

VIRGINIA I'm . . . a girl, John, truly.

JOHN PRYNNE That's common sense, isn't it?

VIRGINIA Sense is not very common, I'm afraid.

JOHN PRYNNE Splendid, very witty!
Where'd you get that from?

VIRGINIA From our teacher at the tech.
He's rather clever, actually.
Most impressive.

I can see the truth, very clear,
Like . . . like glass,
Like looking in a looking-glass.

JOHN PRYNNE I don't get you.

VIRGINIA You couldn't care for me as a person, could you,
Well, not really?
Someone . . . who looks at me, and I look at them,
A person needs a person,
Not love, it doesn't have to be that, John,
Just . . . you know . . .

JOHN PRYNNE . . . I know that, don't I?

I'm very shy.
That's my trouble,
To be quite frank for a moment.
You should be sorry for me in fact,
Not trying to hurt me,
Trying to get me down,
Trying to make me feel so low.

I've never known a nice girl, like you.
A really nice one.

VIRGINIA To be quite frank,
I don't trust you.

JOHN PRYNNE Why not, for god's sake?
Have I cheated you?
Have I let you down?
You've got nothing against me, have you?
What are you accusing me of, exactly?
Let's have it quickly,
And get it over!

VIRGINIA I don't like you really.
I can't help it.

It's nothing personal, truly.

(*Taking his hand.*) I thought you were my . . . don't laugh, will
you? . . . true love . . . when you followed me that
day . . . I thought, my, he's keen! . . . what's got
into him? . . . I thought when you stopped me you
liked me truly . . . and the way you fought that
fancy fella for me . . . so I agreed to see you . . . I
thought you might turn out kind and charming . . .
well, *galante*, and longing for me deeply, courting
me with little gifts and flowers, like I said . . . I'm
so romantic . . .
. . . with no hard words or cruel talking . . . just
peace like birds . . . and go walking . . . and walk
hand in hand . . . with a smile in our hearts . . .
being young at the moment . . .

JOHN PRYNNE It's all so childish,
The way you talk,
The way you carry on.
*He puts his arm around her, and tries to tug her
towards him.*

VIRGINIA I don't like you, see,
That's all.
They kiss. She begins to struggle. They go on kissing,
JOHN PRYNNE *insisting.*

SCENE SIX

ROSIE BRACKLEY, *buxom, capacious and warm, in a tasteless housecoat, convalescent.* STRONG *has finished his examination, and, back to her, is putting his implements away in a bag. She gesticulates to* VIRGINIA, *who puts down a cheap tray, on which there is a bottle of dessert wine, and a single glass.* VIRGINIA *smiles at her mother, and before leaving touches her mother's hair and housecoat, solicitously, kindly.*

VIRGINIA You look lovely, mother.

ROSIE Sssh!

Clear off now.

Exit VIRGINIA.

O, doctor.

A glass of wine before you go, doctor!

She giggles.

STRONG Rosie, Rosie,

I must be on my way, dear.

The quick and the dead call out.

Heh-heh. May I?

ROSIE O doctor!

The way the words trip off your tongue.

Pour yourself a little glass, go on then.

STRONG Avoid melancholy, Rosie,

Let us act our parts bravely, eh?

Splendid, splendid!

She giggles.

ROSIE O doctor!

You're a real tonic, you are!

You're very experienced, you are, doctor,

I can tell.

The way you squeeze my hands, you lovely man!

STRONG (*pouring another glass*).

And all shall be well,

And all manner of things shall be well!

I thirst, he said, on the cross. Aagh!

Splendid, splendid!

ROSIE So . . . so easy and gay you are, the things you do.

You're . . . you're life to me, you are!

STRONG Ah, the happy tears roll down your buxom cheek.

Heh-heh, eh, Rosie?

ROSIE You've gotta real faith in your eye, doctor,

I'm always telling Arthur, and 'Ginia,

A sort of glimmer of god,

I dunno . . .

STRONG . . . O loving heart!

Love is a woman's all,

Is it not, Rosie?

STRONG *pours another drink.*

ROSIE A sort of shining light,

A kind of radiance really,

So strong you are, and simple,

You believe in god, don't you, doctor?

I can tell, Rosie knows you know, doctor.

STRONG Christ, the child, I saw, hanging on a woman's breast!

She emits a little scream, and draws her housecoat together.

Christ, the man, hanging on a bloody tree!

ROSIE Oh, my gawd!

I feel so shivery when I hear you talk.

All in a fever, flushing all over.

(*In his ear.*) I must be very ill.

She giggles.

STRONG Nothing that love can't cure,

A spouse's close embrace,

48

A hairy paw!
She screams and laughs, seizing his hand, her
housecoat opening.
We must all grow from fear to love, my dear,
That's it, that's it.
STRONG *frees himself.*

ROSIE O doctor!
My husband . . . I shouldn't say, really,
It's a betrayal, I feel ashamed already,
Him so trusting,
Trying hard, he does, try, doctor,
Arthur does try really . . .

STRONG . . . Drink to me only!

ROSIE . . . But it ain't no good, doctor,
I mean . . . he ought to . . .
And him leaving so early . . .
I never . . . well you know . . .
I like it in the morning . . .
She giggles.
. . . He's so tired and pasty,
Me waiting here,
Loving really, well I do,
Loving really!
O doctor, I got so much love in me,
I'm bursting!
STRONG *drinks hurriedly.*

STRONG Pray to god, Rosie.
God is love at the last,
When all else fails.
To believe in god, it is not necessary to know for
certain that he exists, my dear.

ROSIE That ain't no good, doctor,
And well you know it.

STRONG Open your heart to him, my dear.
Let him enter into you!

D   49

ROSIE *laughs*.

Yield your soul up to him.

ROSIE You wicked creature!

STRONG Your pills before I go.

ROSIE You're very experienced you are, doctor!

Don't go, yet, doctor.

Please!

STRONG A sweet morsel under your tongue,

And these up your back passage.

I'll call again. Good day!

ROSIE O doctor!

The shame of it!

How could you!

Me a woman like I am,

To talk so common.

Ah, doctor, what a shame!

You've got no respect.

To talk like that.

And me . . . so gentle to you.

Just fancy!

STRONG The doctor's round, my dear.

It's sad I know,

But there it is. Enough now.

ROSIE . . . Life being so short, and all.

STRONG We must steal hours from the night,

To lengthen our days, dear Rosie.

And so, farewell.

ROSIE Perhaps you aren't so wise, Doctor know-all,

You and your dear Rosie!

Some of our days and nights are all used up, aren't
they,

Living to work,

No life for him or me, take Arthur,

On the knocker, a bloody slave for eighteen bloody
quid a week . . .

STRONG . . . Wealth cannot turn ugliness into beauty!! . . .

ROSIE Travelling around so free,
   Poking up all our bodies to your heart's content,
   When we got no lives to speak of,
   Or nothing a person can be proud of, really!
   Look at me, doctor!
   I had me life once, didn't I, you remember,
   Now I'm just a housewife, rotting here all lonely,
   And me poor hubby's gone to seed, poor fellow,
   The world all rotten and so cruel.

STRONG We must bear up beneath it all,
   And be resolute in hope and will.
   And now forgive me.

ROSIE It's just words, doctor.
   It's just your bedside talk,
   Tell your Rosie,
   You don't mean it, do you,
   You don't understand.
   I'm not just a nice body.
   I gotta heart, and soul, inside me.

STRONG You're all right, my dear.
   You're fine, fine,
   A fine woman.
   After Rubens.
   As right as rain.
   Of course you are, Rosie.
   The figure of the world,
   Of the Earth, our mother,
(*Swaying.*) Of course you are, Rosie.

ROSIE I'm just another case to you.
   I'm not a person,
   I've got my symptoms.
   That's all you want to know.

STRONG We are all bodies, Rosie.
   I too.

Sensations of rapturous heat, and sighs – I know them.

There's a secret I confide in you.

ROSIE I'm different.

I'm Rosie.

I want to feel . . . different.

I want to . . . feel a different person.

STRONG You have your . . . beauty still.

ROSIE Beauty's only skin deep, mister.

STRONG Deep enough for most of your species.

ROSIE No.

It isn't deep enough for me.

See?

I want beauty in me life.

I want it to be . . . sort of radiant, truly radiant.

STRONG It's the perpetual dropping that wears away the stone.

O how to lighten our burdens, eh, Rosie?

ROSIE You understand very little,

I'm afraid to say.

STRONG Splendid, splendid!

How to prolong life, eh?

How to be spared headaches?

How to feel happy, eh?

ROSIE No, doctor, no!

STRONG There are no return tickets issued on this line.

ROSIE That's just talking for the sake of talking.

STRONG What counts is to be in the world.

That's a rich consolation!

ROSIE (*seizing his lapels*).

You liar!

You cheat!

You 'ypocrite!!

STRONG Ah, Rosie, flower of fire and wrath!

ROSIE I'm not in one of those female frenzies,
  Don't you start thinking that,
  Hysterical this and that,
  Neurotic and all,
  That's all you doctors can think of,
  Hungry housewives, panting for men,
  Well we ain't, see!
  So keep your hands off me,
  Drinking all our bloody muscatel,
  My poor husband out working, all this woe
  and sorrow, and pains in his heart,
  Me so treacherous, and him so trusting,
  Treason that's what it is,
  And I'm deadly calm,
  I've got a grown-up daughter,
  I'm telling you,
  I can see it all dead clear,
  And you'll never know, degrees and all!!!
  ROSIE *sobbing*, VIRGINIA *peeping*.
STRONG The paschal lamb is eaten with bitter herbs.
  Mirandum dei opus, god's masterpiece,
  Signatura rerum. Fools have the first word, women
  the last.
  A silence. Sobbing. STRONG *has a quick drink.*
ROSIE I'm sorry,
  But you're a fine sort of lover, ain't you, doctor,
  Mumbling on, blinding me with science, all fancy,
  Me sitting here,
  Offering meself to you, well I was before,
  And you couldn't see.
  I'm all . . . humiliated,
  Telling you me all, a stranger,
  Giving you body and heart and soul.
  Go away.
  I feel very faint because of you.

STRONG I am escaped with the skin of my teeth.
Hippocrates calls.

ROSIE I'm living a dying sort of life,
Full of . . . emptiness.
But I'll find my love and beauty.
Oh yes, I will.

STRONG Be merry and strong, my dear.
It is better to bear your own troubles, than to worry
others with them.

ROSIE It's easier to look wise,
Than to talk wisdom, mister,
You liars are only cowards,
There's lots more slop from the same pail, ain't there?
You dish it out, oh yes!
Exploiting us, another bloody exploiter!
Always saying those smooth things, and saying
them easy.

ROSIE turns her back on STRONG.

Size yourself up, doctor,
You're not so young,
Step back and take a look sometime.

STRONG Is this a festival,
Or a funeral?!!
You tell me!!

ROSIE A festival, my love,
If you're nice and kind.

Exit STRONG.

'Corse it is, if you've got a smile in your heart, that's
all.
I'm sorry, doctor.

ROSIE sees STRONG *has gone.*

My hubby's coming home soon, poor fella,
And me undressed,
Showing all meself like this.

.   .   .

54

Lovely man, that doctor.
She begins to cry.
Cruel fellow!

SCENE SEVEN

A club, a confined space, a platform, a mike, lurid lighting, youths and girls, a slow gyration of legs and arms, breasts and buttocks, gently bucking and bending, music, a band, roaring. Among them the black youth, SAMMY dancing, then shouting. Only TERRY, sullen, in leather jacket, watches. VIRGINIA is one of the girls, hanging back.

SAMMY Blood me black,
        Children of the world!
VOICES Go man, go!
SAMMY Blood me black,
        Children of the world!
ANNIE Get the scene going!
SAMMY Pump that piano, yeh!
        Pump it hard,
        And pump me out a beautiful dream!
        He leaps on to the platform, and seizes the mike.
ANNIE Tell us who's where, Sammy,
        Who's going there!
SAMMY Pump that piano,
        And pump it fast,
        And pump me out,
        Some black and white cream!
        Screaming, dancing.
VOICES Get the scene going!

SAMMY O.K., kids,
> This is the happening scene!
> I'm . . . licking my thick blue lips, man!
> *Screams.*
> A black boy's starting your storm, man!

ANNIE Get the scene going!
> TERRY *tries to interfere, and is pushed away.*

SAMMY I'm licking my thick blue lips, man,
> I don't want no more white tips, man,
> I'm rocking your knives and forks, man,
> And I'm gonna pop your corks!
> *Screams and laughter.*

GIRLS Sammy, Sammy!

SAMMY My legs are snapping like twigs . . .

VOICES . . . Go, man, go!

SAMMY I'm puffing my hash in cigs . . .
> . . . My pink mouth is goin' dry, man,
> I'm fixing to make you cry, man,
> Mary Joanna!

VOICES Mary Joanna!
> TERRY *tries to seize* SAMMY.
> *The former is grabbed, felled, and kicked, while the
> dancing and music roar on.*

SAMMY Cut me an album on my wrist, man,
> Dip the snow and clench my fist, man . . .

VOICES Mary Joanna!
> ANNIE *crying out, trying to get on to the platform.*

SAMMY . . . Sucking you in little sips,
> I'm goin' on one o' my trips,
> I'm turnin' on so fast,
> I'm gonna make it last . . .

VOICES Mary Joanna!

ANNIE (*clutching* SAMMY).
> Wild man, wild man, go!
> You're fun to be with,

Crazy to talk with,
You make me go!
Laughter; she takes off her glasses, shakes out her hair.

VOICES Ask him for it! She's asking for it!

ANNIE Do me a favour, man,
Give me your flavour, man,
Make me go!
SAMMY *grabs her.*
Touch my little button,
And make me go!

VOICES Mary Joanna!

SAMMY Give me your heart, babe,
And I'll shoot up your chart, babe,
I'll walk you in the sky, babe,
I'll teach you to fly so high, babe!
All gather round, clapping rhythmically.
We're the gooniest and looniest ever,
We're on a crazy merry-go-round!

ALL Moody Blues,
Beach Boys,
Moody Blues,
Bee-gees,
D.J., P.J.,
Top stars, pop stars,
Mary Joanna!

ANNIE I'm a goo,
I'm swooning,
I'm a goo!

ALL Moody Blues,
Beach Boys,
Moody Blues,
Bee-gees,
Mary Joanna!
Pout-pout,
Kiss-kiss!

57

ANNIE I'm a goo!
They kiss.
This is the big scene, Sammy.

SAMMY Rocker-dolly,
Pretty-polly,
Let me suck you,
With my deep blue lips.

ANNIE Oh, clear the deck,
And travel me light!

ALL Kiss-kiss!
Underwhelm me,
Overwhelm me!

ALL Pretty boy, pretty boy.

ANNIE Tell me to do it, pretty boy, pretty boy,
Slowly, slowly.

ALL Slowly, slowly!

ANNIE Star me, spin me,
Namaste, namaste,
Flower me! Flower me!
They sink down. Soft music.
The crowd watches.

LOUISA Tiger Boy!
Tiger Baby!
(*Screaming.*) Feel me tight,
Feel me close!!

GIRLS Sammy!
The girls struggle with each other, and try to drag
ANNIE *away.*

LOUISA See me, Sammy,
Say hello to me, Sammy,
Read me, fill me, knock me down!
TERRY *tries to seize her.*
Go away, stinky, pinky boy!
Tugging at SAMMY.
Take me, take me!

58

TERRY *tries to grab* SAMMY.
Fighting. Music.

SAMMY This ain't your scene, punk man,
This ain't your scene!
Uproar.
Get the real scene going!
Mind blowing! Black crowing!
Dig me, shake me,
Hot line shoot me,
Get things going out of your mind!

TERRY (*spitting*).
Nigger!

ANNIE Break him!
Kick him!

SAMMY I'll clench my fist, and bust the charts, man,
And you can come smell real, black, farts, man!
My legs are snapping like sticks.
(*Seizing* TERRY.) I got you in a fix.
I'll suck you with my lips,
My mouth is going dry,
I'm gonna make you cry,
Mary Joanna!
The crowd gathers around TERRY, *kicking him.*
I'm the gooniest and looniest ever,
I'm on a crazy merry-go-round!
Screams. TERRY *covers his face. Blood.*
Cut man, cut.
Stop the scene,
Stop it rolling.
Cut!
Dog-face is crying, man.
Too bad, man, too bad.

TERRY Nigger!!

ANNIE Sammy!

SAMMY I'm gonna find out what you wanna do, dog face.

I wanna look into you, man,
And find out what you wanna do.
Eh, man?

TERRY Nigger!
The crowd jeers at TERRY. *He lashes them away.*

SAMMY You answer me a few questions, dog-face!
Which soul singing-star died in Lake Monona,
In a big splash down, eh, man?

TERRY Nigger!

SAMMY Who was Otis Redding?

TERRY Nigger!

SAMMY Who was Jimmy King?

TERRY Nigger!

SAMMY Who is the champion of the world?

TERRY Nigger!

ANNIE Don't, Sammy!

SAMMY Who am I?
You tell me quick, sir,
You tell me quick!

TERRY Nigger!!
A silence.

LOUISA You're only jealous! I hate you, Terry, now, I hate
you!
'Cos he's the grooviest, fabbest, excitingest,
smashingest, superbest boy in the world!
Come on, Sammy!
Don't be hurt, Sammy!
Get the scene going, Sammy!
The kids are asking for it!

SAMMY Are we gonna rave for ever?

ALL Yes!

SAMMY Then, go, man, go!
Get the scene going!
This is the happening scene!
The dance begins again, bucking, bending, gyrating.

SCENE EIGHT

ROSS *and* ROSIE *in* STRONG's *surgery waiting-room.*
A gay and garrulous conversation is in mid-flight.
ROSIE, *florid, overdressed, blowsy;* ROSS, *white and*
addled, older.

ROSIE I've got insight, the doctor says,
We're very confidential.
She laughs.
He likes my figure,
Of course I've got a grown-up daughter,
He's got taste, he sees beauty.

Actually, I shouldn't say,
I lost my heart to him, in my sickness,
Once upon a time.
Never mind, a lovely man he is, professional, really.

He didn't lay a finger, well only in the course of
duty, you know.

You're a teacher then, are you, yes, I thought so.
Always tell a teacher.

My hubby's a postman, poor bugger,
A lifetime on the knocker,
'Corse he's had a coronary thrombosis, just recent,
Gone very pasty,
What with blue lips and puffy ankles, you know,
He ain't so good.
Still, that's life, ain't it?

I dunno what men are,
I dunno what they're worth, really.

Terrible fighting in the papers.

What I say is, black and white together,
We're all brothers,
Little lambs they are,
Well, black sheep really.
Fighting, well, it sets people back,
Sets them back in learning,
Of course, pardon me, you'd know all that,
wouldn't you . . .

. . . Being a teacher.
You said a teacher?
Prob'ly you had my daughter.
'Corse she's done her schooling,
I've forgotten all about it.
We don't see her much,
Now she's working, living independent.
They don't tell you.
I got Arthur.

He's my hubby.
He's got coronary thrombosis.
Gone very pasty.
What with blue lips and puffy ankles,
He ain't so good,
Still that's life, ain't it?
What's wrong with you then?

ROSS Inertia.

ROSIE Really.
My hubby had that once.
Very painful.

(*Giggling.*) He wears a truss now.
  Lifting them heavy postbags, early one morning.

  I'm not a coquette.
  Don't start thinking.
  I'm a lady.
  You don't look sick, not really.
ROSS My disease is fatal.
ROSIE How romantic!
  You might be a dying poet,
  Coughing out yer water-wings,
  With tuberculosis.
ROSS I fashion nothing.
  I am no maker!
ROSIE You've got neurosis.
  Your type's always got neurosis.
  Thumbs in yer bums,
  And yer minds in neutral,
  Arthur says.
  Poor fella.
  I bet that's you all over.
ROSS Correct,
  I am a teacher.
ROSIE Don't think that excuses you, mister!
  He moves a seat nearer.
  I'm not filled with wonder.
  I might have been once,
  When my life was radiant.
  You've got no beauty.
ROSS Absolutely not! Heh-heh!
ROSIE You're not a serious person.
  A silence.
ROSS You're rather unusual . . .
ROSIE . . . Don't start to patronize me, neither.
ROSS You have a certain elemental vigour.

> I find it increasingly curious,
> Identifying the mainsprings of action . . .

ROSIE . . . Come off it.
> I know what yer after,
> Your type,
> Intellectual.
> We're all bodies, mister,
> You as well,
> So don't come all the blarney.
> I've got what you want, haven't I?
> That's all there is to it.
> You're all so bloody boring.
> I've got a grown-up daughter.

ROSS So what?

ROSIE I'm a respectable person,
> That's what.

ROSS Do you seriously think I . . .

ROSIE . . . Yes, sir. I do.

ROSS What fatuity, or vanity,
> I can't determine which.

ROSIE Determine which?
> Come off it,
> You bloody softies,
> I prefer my Arthur,
> He's got guts, he has.

ROSS I'm sure he has, indeed.

ROSIE Some men make roads,
> Others walk on them.
> You're one of those who walks on them, mister.
> One of these fellows who starts at the top,
> And works his way to the bottom, aren't you?

ROSS A continuous regression.

ROSIE Why don't you speak simple!
> It's exploitation,
> Speak some truth, man.

64

ROSS   What is truth,
      But the longest lie?
ROSIE   Baloney.
      Where's yer duty?
      You want to meditate, really.
      That's the thing.
      I've been reading it in the papers.
ROSS   I've got too much to think about to meditate,
      madam.
ROSIE   That's a good one,
      Too much to think about to meditate, yes,
      You've said it there, you've said it quite finely.

      It's a pity you're not fine and manly, though.
ROSS   From the rear, I am fit for the obscene kiss.
ROSIE   I dunno what you mean, and I'm not asking.
      Try again.

      You want to speak more natural.

      Money talks, doesn't it?
ROSS   Poverty also.
ROSIE   No one wants to hear what it has to say, do they?
      My hubby's only got his pension.
      We need a bloody revolution!
      You wouldn't know, would ya,
      Stuck with your shiny grey backside in some fat
      armchair,
      Your little white feet in felt slippers,
      Your big arse croaking like a bloody frog in
      summer.
      I can see you!
      ROSS *comes a chair nearer.*
ROSS   I'm in hiding.
      I know nothing.

Would you rather a bird's beak, or a bullock's
buttocks?

ROSIE (*giggling*).

How disgusting!

ROSS I can waste time without anxiety.

ROSIE Don't kid yourself!

What the hell are you here for?

ROSS Doing nothing is more serious than work.

ROSIE Git!

And I suppose you go round criticizing other
people.

ROSS When I choose. What's wrong with that?

ROSIE Well you've got no right, mister.

You've only got a right to criticize,

If you've got the heart to help.

ROSS Not so. A trick, not the truth.

A man must be uninvolved,

To judge with reason.

ROSIE (*blowing a raspberry*).

You sound very clever,

Like the bloody doctor, degrees and that,

You too, the wonders of bleeding education.

He'd've led me up the garden, I'm telling you,

If I hadn't've spotted a phoney,

Calling me darling a long time ago now, and all that
jazz, so hurtful.

It just isn't truthful with a person.

A silence. ROSS *takes her hand.*

Have you no guilt doing this to a married woman?

ROSS None at all,

None whatsoever.

ROSIE You're naughty.

ROSS Better to sin than be sinned against.

He puts his hand on her leg.

ROSIE What do you believe in then?
ROSS (*moving his hand*).
Have little to do,
And do it yourself.
ROSIE But you're a teacher.
Don't you care?
ROSS No.
Why should I? It's a soft option.
ROSIE You're naughty,
Really.
I could like you.
In a way,
It's very peculiar.
Have you no guilt with a married lady?
ROSS No.
ROSIE How charming!

You only want to use me, don't you?
ROSS Yes.
ROSIE I could use you, darling.
Aren't we naughty?
ROSS It depends on what you mean exactly.
ROSIE You're bloody right, darling!

I've got migraine.
ROSS I've got an ulcer.

Let's go, shall we?
ROSIE Yes, come on then.
ROSS What's your name?
ROSIE My name is Rosie.

What's yours?
ROSS Tom . . . Gilbert.
ROSIE I don't believe it.

What does it matter?

It doesn't matter, does it, darling?

SCENE NINE

In the window of a boutique, naked female dummies are being dressed by a girl in tights, TERESA. *Passing,* LAWRENCE PRYNNE, *even sprucer than before, with orchid button-hole, gold-topped cane, and monocled eye, silk ruffled shirt, and, almost immobilized, limping in tight trousers. He has a blond wig, and dyed moustache. He passes the window, and goes off. He returns, as if casually, examines a fob-watch, and takes a pill. A second girl,* VIRGINIA, *in tights, joins the first in the window. The two girls talk animatedly.*

PRYNNE They talk together in low voices.
They find me absurd.
So be it.
The girls dance in the window.
Is it fair to dance and sing,
When death's bells ring,
Eh?

What else but sex do you?!!
What else?
You are nothing more than passages!
VIRGINIA What?
Come again, mister!
PRYNNE Passages!!!
Passages for food and sex,

Manufacturers of dung,
Fillers-up of privies!
Nothing else will remain of you,
But full privies!
You shall perish for ever, like your own dung!!
VIRGINIA What?
PRYNNE (*sadly*).
I'm dying, but you are dead.
Boys and girls of the world,
Children of fools!

(*Striking window Sinful amusement,
with stick*). School of vice!

Flee lust,
Watch and pray,
Turn with disgust.
O help me, help me!
The woman catches the precious soul of a man!
Laughter within.
Woe to them that laugh, for they shall weep!
Tears shall flow beyond the grave.
They shall be shed in purgatory, they shall be shed in hell.
O, cut off the part that torments the soul,
Pluck out the eye that is a source of sin.

(*Furtively.*) A glance as quick as thought.
Ah, sweet shape. I melt like a fool.
Tights.
Bum.
So be it.
Grace and form.
A stage, a dance, a play.
A decent play is well enough,

But where do you find decent plays today?
See.
They move.
They bend. Look!
My heart barks.
My heart breaks.

LOUISA *and* TERRY *approach the shop.*

Eschew vanity in dress, my dears!
Be pure in mind, in thought, desire and deed!

LOUISA Come on, Terry, he's a nut.

TERRY What's he saying?

LOUISA Come all ye faithful, prob'ly.
Quick!

They enter the shop. The dressers leave the window.

PRYNNE (*looking at his reflection*).
Not a sign of senescence.
Dapper still.
The pills a wonder.

Time and motion, I.
(*Twirling stick.*) Here I go,
See me go.
I shall take my life in my teeth.
The root of the matter is found in me.
Love is all technique.
Late in life, I learn the truth, friends.
It's all technique! Heh-heh.
Age thus has the edge on youth.
Love is this and that.
Sweet nothings.

PRYNNE *tries to do a rap routine; fails, panting, limping.*

Never a body without fault.
I too, not made right, down below.
I am a lemon which has been sucked dry.

So be it.
Doctor Strong will see me through.
And what is love, friends, I ask you?

A lover only dotes on flesh and blood, on meat and
bone, and a ha'p'orth of gristle.
More fool he, or she, as the case may be.
Eh?
Heh-heh!
The dressers and shoppers stare out, grinning at
PRYNNE.

(*Pointing at dummy*
with stick.) What is . . . a gently rounded face,
Soft azure eyes,
A slender neck,
A supple shoulder,
And a luxurious breast?
Look, friends, look!
What is a tapering waist,
And swelling thigh, I ask you,
And delicate feet and hands?
What is a rose and lily tint,
And soft fine auburn hair?
The dressers and shoppers emerge from the shop to
watch.
What are they, what are they, I ask you,
The admirable mammae,
What are they?

(*Pointing to*
VIRGINIA.) The admirable mammae,
What are they, you tell me,
Rising and curving on every side?
Are they as pendant as gravity demands, eh?
What is the flexile waist,

Tapering to the middle of the trunk,
I ask you?

What is this flat expanse between the hips,
A dimple on either side?
You tell me, you tell me!
Does it slope gently to the mount of love, eh, really,
I ask you, I ask you!

Answer me, what are they, what are they?!!
PRYNNE *seizes* TERESA. *A tug of war,* PRYNNE
striking with his stick.
From the top of the head, to the roots of the hair,
From the root of the hair to the eyebrows,
From the eyebrows to the bottom of your nose,
What are you?

TERRY Lay off 'er, you bleedin' nut, I'll do you!

LOUISA It's O.K., Terry, he's harmless, leave him.
TERESA *breaks away.*

PRYNNE From the bottom of the nose to the chin,
From the chin to the breast bone,
From the breast bone to the base of your little
breast, what are you?
Laughter. Exeunt TERRY *and* LOUISA.
From the base of the breast to the navel,
And from the navel to your mount of love, what
are you?

(*To himself.*) From . . . the mount of love, to the kneck of the leg,
From the kneck of the leg to the knee,
From the knee to the calf,
From the calf to the ankle,
From the ankle to the tips of your little toes,
What are you?
Eh, my dear, what are you?

Tell me. I ask you.

THE DRESSERS We're girls, sir.

PRYNNE Girls?

And what else but sex do you?!

They giggle.

What else, my dears?

THE DRESSERS We go dancing.

PRYNNE Is that not . . . sexual also?

They giggle.

THE DRESSERS You must be daft.

We like to enjoy ourselves, don't we?

What's wrong with that?

PRYNNE Dancing . . . leads to every sort of vice.

It can do, really.

It sullies the purity of the heart.

THE DRESSERS Don't talk such bloody baloney.

You don't know what you're talking about.

You're having us on.

You're a bit dirty.

PRYNNE Does not . . . dancing give rise to jealousy?

TERESA Of course not.

VIRGINIA Well sometimes.

PRYNNE To jokes and quarrels?

And cruelties?

THE DRESSERS No, silly!

PRYNNE To . . . to voluptuous desires?

THE DRESSERS That's what we go for!

PRYNNE (*quietly*).

To bold words,

And caresses,

Licentious looks,

Lewd glances?

THE DRESSERS Oo, yes, it's lovely!

PRYNNE Young men and women in each other's arms,

73

> The excitement of the music,
> Strong drinks and drugs and flimsy clothes,
> High spirits, and a whirl of talk,
> And what have you, my friends?

THE DRESSERS A bloody good rave-up, mister!

PRYNNE (*sadly*).

> And after the dance,
> The dancer sees his partner home,
> They both excited.
> In the dark, in solitary places,
> With passions kindled,
> The precious crown of purity is lost,
> The treasure taken!
> Is that not so?
> Is it not often as I say?

TERESA Oo yes, sir, yes, sir!

VIRGINIA Don't be so nosey!

PRYNNE Ha!

> As I thought!
> (*Fiercely*.) Under the bushes you bray like asses,
> Trodden from behind!!

VIRGINIA You old fellas are all the same,

> Because you're past it, I've seen fellas
> like you before,
> You never have it,
> So you want to stop us having it,
> It's a free country, ain't it?

PRYNNE Pah!

TERESA What've you got that any one'd want?

> Eh?
> Your fancy clothes and all that flounce!
> Where does it get you, eh?

VIRGINIA Taking pills,

> To make you go,
> To pep you up,

It makes us sick!

PRYNNE I cannot withdraw my words.
Reflect that while you dance and sing,
Men writhe in torment!
They jeer.
(*Strutting.*) Illness stalks the earth.
Reflect that while you play,
You dance towards eternity, my dears.
They laugh, and run away.
Flee from sins!
(*Looking at watch.*) Watch and pray!
Let not sorrow come too late.
He that loves danger shall perish in it,
As surely as night follows day!

All that is in the world is the desire of the flesh,
And the pride of life.
Slay the enemy,
And save the soul, friends!

(*Quietly.*) The vexation of a dream!
A girl I've seen before.
That she should forget me!
What sadness!

Oh, sweet shape! The little prettinesses of your
body!
A pause.
I shall overcome!
A pause.
It is not too late.
It can be done.

SCENE TEN

ROSIE, *girlish, virginal, innocent in manner and dress,
seated, sipping tea, faces the visiting* VIRGINIA,
*brash, brassy, confident in manner and dress; chewing
gum and cocky, in a coat, and microscopic skirt.*

VIRGINIA Yeh. Sure I let him.
   He wasn't the first.
  ROSIE Who was 'the first'?
VIRGINIA That Johnny fella.
   That bloody, jumped-up clerk, you remember.
  ROSIE Where? When?
VIRGINIA That horrible fella I hated.
   On the bleeding sofa!
   Right here!
  ROSIE (*getting off sofa*).
   I've a good mind to tell my husband. You've gone
   all promiscuous.
   I lived my life for you.

   You've lost your flower.
VIRGINIA In bunches.
  ROSIE Oh.
   How disgraceful!

   On this sofa?
VIRGINIA Yeh.
  ROSIE (*sitting down again*).
   How could you!
VIRGINIA Shall I tell you?
   You wanna know how I did it?
  ROSIE Please!

76

I'm your mother.

VIRGINIA How're yah doing?

Got a lover?

ROSIE *screams.*

ROSIE Your father's had a coronary thrombosis.

VIRGINIA You must have, then. Is he useless?

ROSIE Virginia!

What's come over you?

VIRGINIA Don't come all this innocent.

I know what you're up to.

ROSIE Your father's been promoted.

VIRGINIA What is he, postmaster bloody general?

ROSIE He's a sorter.

VIRGINIA Poor bugger.

ROSIE Virginia!

Have you . . . have you . . .

VIRGINIA Yeh?

ROSIE . . . got a boy friend?

VIRGINIA I'm shacked up with a fella.

You could call him a boy friend.

ROSIE Does he respect you?

VIRGINIA He has me. We get along mostly, sort of.

ROSIE O Virginia!

VIRGINIA Yeh?

ROSIE O Virginia!

(*Dabbing her eyes.*) They made my husband a sorter,

And then he got this coronary thrombosis,

It changed his life.

He's such a nice person really.

You did hurt him, going away without saying.

You were so cruel.

VIRGINIA Are you guilty or something?

ROSIE Guilty? Me?

VIRGINIA Crying.

77

       Got something on your conscience, eh?

ROSIE Me?

       Of course not.

       It's you I'm talking about,

       Going off, not saying goodbye,

       Like a . . . like a . . . flibberty-gibbet,

       Giving us all this worry.

VIRGINIA O gawd, spare me!

ROSIE What've you been doing?

VIRGINIA I've been around.

ROSIE Have you been working?

VIRGINIA Off and on, sort of.

ROSIE How've you been earning? Eh?

VIRGINIA It's all been legal.

ROSIE I see.

       Not . . . ?

VIRGINIA No!

       Mother!!

ROSIE O Virginia!

       You want to be . . .

       . . . you want to be . . .

VIRGINIA . . . Yeh?

ROSIE More chaste!

       There.

       I said it.

       It ain't good for you.

       You were a lovely person.

       The apple of your mother's eye.

VIRGINIA Stop. For christ's sake!

ROSIE You've got no beauty.

       You've lost it. It shows on you.

VIRGINIA Worry about yourself, ma, you're older.

ROSIE Brought up nice you were,

       Fat lot you care,

It breaks my heart talking.

Your father will be most upset.

VIRGINIA How ya doing with my old teacher?

ROSIE (*simpering, whispering*).
Virginia!

VIRGINIA Just good friends, eh?

ROSIE Yes, we are.

He's an intellectual.

VIRGINIA What's he been teaching you?

ROSIE Please!
I won't have it!

VIRGINIA What are you learning then, ma?
Eh?
Won't you tell your lovely daughter?

ROSIE He's . . . rather charming.
It's not a secret. What do you know about it, Virginia?

VIRGINIA What does your husband think of it, eh, then?

ROSIE That's my business.
And don't speak so loud.
He's sleeping.

He's an agnostic.

VIRGINIA I thought Dad was a bloody tory.

ROSIE I mean . . . Mr Ross is.
I mean . . . how does one know?
Can one be certain?

VIRGINIA He's giving you the run round.
You want to be careful.
Losing yer flower.

ROSIE He's very experienced.
He knows how to respect a woman.
He needs me.

79

VIRGINIA Oh, mother!
  (*Gently.*) How could you! He's so . . . lazy.
             He's not much to look at, is he?
             He's ugly really.
  ROSIE Maybe.

(*Taking her hand.*) He makes me happy. He makes me happy.
           VIRGINIA *withdraws her hand.*
           I'm your mother, aren't I?!
           ROSIE *seizes* VIRGINIA *convulsively, the latter struggling to free herself, crying out.*

SCENE ELEVEN

LAWRENCE PRYNNE, *in a dark suit, stripped of embellishment, without a toupee, pale, ill, is being helped into a chair by* STRONG.

STRONG We have the results of your tests, Prynne.

        You're dying! I'm so sorry.
PRYNNE (*gripping hold of* STRONG).
        Don't leave me, doctor.
STRONG To the devil with you!
        Your next of kin can phone me.
PRYNNE There's nothing wrong with me!
        You're joking!
        O Mother Mary!
        I am suffering from gout, that's it, that's what it is,
        Isn't it, doctor,
        I've got gout,
        You tell me of the tests afterwards, won't you, sir,

I am suffering from gout,
I cannot put my foot on the ground, sir.
A silence.

(*Struggling with*
STRONG.) You're joking!
Tell me, doctor!!!

STRONG God will not carry away a perfect man like you,
Prynne, will he?

PRYNNE He will not, sir.

I plan to work, sir.
I want a job.
My past life is over.
I am chaste again in mind and body.
My course of sin is over.

(*Screaming.*) I'm not dying, doctor!!
A silence : PRYNNE *falls down.*
Am I?
A silence ; PRYNNE *crawling; clutching* STRONG's
legs.

STRONG I pity you, Prynne.
Make terms with death now.
Man should not cringe and fawn.
Maintain a calm courage, and you will have my
sympathy.

PRYNNE What are you saying?

STRONG (*pouring a drink*).
This is the sublime pathos of human life.

PRYNNE What are you saying?
I'm dying.

STRONG In the drinking of a glass of wine,
My heart is lifted higher.

PRYNNE Doctor, help me!
Be my friend!

STRONG To be the friend of everyone is not possible, my
       good fellow!
       All is illness for the time being.

PRYNNE Speak to me,
       Don't leave me! Pluck me from the gate of
       death ...

STRONG I am weary for the pure springs of thought.

PRYNNE I too, sir,
       Believe me, believe me!
       I'm dying!

STRONG My spirit is equal to the entire cosmos,
       To earth and ocean.

PRYNNE Don't leave me!
       I need you.

STRONG My thought is stronger than the titanic sea,
       And all profundity.
       The story of my heart, Prynne.

PRYNNE It's my life, doctor.
       You owe it to me.
       I'm a man, sir.

STRONG (*drinking*).
       Give me wine and meat
       And length of days!

PRYNNE What about me, sir?
       I worship beauty. Restore my youth, my eagle's
       plumage.

STRONG I too adore beauty, and worship the body,
       But without rancour or regret, Prynne.
       It is splendid to climb the steep green hill,
       And swim in the ocean.

PRYNNE Oh yes, doctor.
       I can harden my body, I can suffer,
       And be strong too.
       Tell me what to do.
       I'm not dying, I know it.

I'm not in any pain really.
It's all baloney, isn't it?
You're just frightening me that's all.
O Mother Mary!
I can deny my body, sir,
That's what you mean, isn't it, doctor?

STRONG No, sir.

PRYNNE I'm beat.
I'm dying.
Save me.

STRONG It is enough to lie on the grass and listen to the song of summer.
That is to be immortal.

PRYNNE But I'm dying.

STRONG O beautiful human life,
Tears come in my eyes as I think of it.
So beautiful,
So inexpressibly beautiful!
PRYNNE *struggles to stand up.*
But if we snatch at our existence, Prynne,
Then our work is as nothing.
How beautiful a delight to make the whole world full of joy . . .

PRYNNE . . . O yes, sir . . .

STRONG . . . The song never silent,
The dance never still.
(*Drinking.*) Water running for ever.
The very thought makes this hour sweet.

PRYNNE But I'm dying, doctor!
You told me!

STRONG The poverty called wealth,
The infamy known as fame,
The building of cities,
The establishments of commerce,

83

All a cipher, worthless fruit, fit only for the birds to peck at.

PRYNNE I want a signing off note, sir.

You've got plenty of money.

I want to work, sir.

STRONG Work is not the main object of existence, Prynne.

It is the lie of a morality founded on money.

Do not confine your mind to the demeaning!

PRYNNE *struggles to his feet.*

PRYNNE Shall I rest then, sir?

Should I rest? Eh? Eh?

STRONG In order to rest, a man must have been occupied.

He who has done nothing, cannot rest.

PRYNNE No sir, no sir,

I'm trying to follow,

I'm impotent doctor, I'm dying,

I don't know what I'm saying.

STRONG I find nothing is of any use,

Unless it gives me a stronger mind and body,

And the happiest existence.

PRYNNE Turn to god, sir, eh?

Is that it, sir?

STRONG There is no directing intelligence in human affairs.

No protection . . .

PRYNNE *struggles to keep his balance.*

. . . And no assistance.

PRYNNE *falls down.* STRONG *turns away.*

(*Drinking.*) Those who act uprightly are seldom rewarded,

Those who do evil go unpunished.

There is a vast immensity of thought and of existence,

And of other things beyond existence.

Tears come into my eyes, Prynne, as I think of it.

But when I consider the fate which overtakes our
little children,
When I consider the depth of man's misery,
I cannot go into my hospital, and face it.
The injured lie bleeding, with none to lift them.

PRYNNE Help me!

STRONG I hear cries louder than thunder,
But none heeds them.
Ears are stopped by the wax of selfishness.

PRYNNE O yes, sir.

STRONG But the mind of man is infinite.
It can understand anything brought before it.
It is the sacred duty of all men to help their
brothers.
That is my delight and pleasure.
That I can lay claim to.

PRYNNE What can I do? Tell me.

STRONG Let me be, in myself, myself fully.

PRYNNE Help me. I'm dying.

STRONG Bad luck, sir.

STRONG *rings his buzzer, for the next patient.*

SCENE TWELVE

STRONG, *and* VIRGINIA *in brassière and knickers,
an examination ending; she attempting to maintain
her blasé exterior.*

STRONG I'm sorry, my dear.
What will you do?

VIRGINIA What the hell does anyone do?

STRONG Will you, ahem . . . ?

85

VIRGINIA . . . That's my business.
I'm not a kid.
Old enough to bleed, old enough to butcher!

Let's have a letter for it then,
Get it over. Please.
STRONG *turns away.*
I'm not going to have it, doctor!
Not bloody likely.
I've got my life to live, haven't I?
Same as anyone.
I'm too young!
Aren't I?

VIRGINIA *dresses, a striptease in reverse: stockings,*
slip, skirt, and blouse.
You can help me. It isn't fair, is it?
I've got myself into trouble, truly, haven't I?

I wasn't . . . sort of . . . expecting to be expecting,
doctor.
Sammy and me always took precautions,
So as not to get me in the family way.
(*Combing her hair.*) It's a crying shame, really.
It's the one that got away, isn't it, doctor,
eh?
Got round the corners, eh, doctor?
It could happen to anyone, couldn't it, doctor?
Please!

What are you looking at me for?
What do you want?
Don't you look at me like that!
STRONG You're shining on me . . . you're . . .

... You shed a fragrance on me.
This little instant will never return again.
Sweet child ... Virginia ... I ... little godsend ...
... Sweet ... innocent child.
VIRGINIA *smacks his face fiercely.*

VIRGINIA Now give us that bleeding letter, mate,
Or else!!
I'll get you struck off, I will,
You bastard!

Aaah, did I hurt you?
There, there, diddums!

Come on, write!!

Write, write, you old bastard!

SCENE THIRTEEN

LAWRENCE PRYNNE *with his son* JOHN. LAWRENCE
PRYNNE *is in a wheelchair, white, gaunt, white-
haired. His son,* JOHN, *is dressing in the style his
father once adopted – in silks and spangles; looking in
a mirror, adjusting his appearance as he painstakingly
goes.*

PRYNNE Taste not, touch not, handle not, my son.
JOHN PRYNNE How does this look, father?
I may not be much to look at, but I'm smartening
myself up, what?
PRYNNE Where are you going?
JOHN PRYNNE Out.

PRYNNE Don't copulate.
Don't masturbate.
Lust grows fat,
Like a beast at pasture.

Don't go, son.
JOHN PRYNNE Jealous?
Eh, father?
PRYNNE You have lots of girls, eh, son? Whores?
It's all technique.
JOHN PRYNNE Here and there. I can have any woman I want now.
It's a great life, if you can manage it.
Be brisk, be virile.
PRYNNE I blew away my life on girls.
JOHN PRYNNE Giving up, at your age? Really!
PRYNNE Why did they wear such clothes?
Why did they smell of scent?
Why did they not really do it?
JOHN PRYNNE Do what?
PRYNNE What they promised.
What they always promised.
They danced through the bright hours,
As I passed.

The smallest sigh,
The sweetest breath,
Moved my old man's monumental heart.
But one dream after another turned to dung.
Opportunities foregone, postponed,
The body wasting, seed cast upon the ground,
The life of Onan.
JOHN PRYNNE You talk as if you were dying.
PRYNNE I am.
Strong told me. The tests.
I am dying.

JOHN PRYNNE You've been dying for the last twenty years, father,
As long as I can remember.

PRYNNE Be good, son. This is my dying fall.
Help others. Be christian.
Simplicity is the shortest cut to morality.

JOHN PRYNNE You're a rogue, dad.
One disguise after another, what? Heh-heh.

PRYNNE Donate your money to good causes.

JOHN PRYNNE Not bally likely.

PRYNNE What about the refugees, the starving? The relief
of famine. Disaster. All that, never ending.

JOHN PRYNNE Their bally problems are their own doing, aren't
they?
They could have prevented them. They don't want
charity.
The wogs don't even try, father.

PRYNNE I'm dying.

JOHN PRYNNE That's right.
You've told me.

PRYNNE You're a nothing.

JOHN PRYNNE Oh really?

PRYNNE You're a nothing.
An unpleasant fellow.
Full of hatred,
Like I was.
Only you've got no reason.

JOHN PRYNNE I've done well, thank you.
You take my money, don't you?
You're one of my good causes.
I'm not complaining.

PRYNNE What is to become of you?

JOHN PRYNNE I'll decide that, if you don't mind.
There's a good fellow.

PRYNNE I don't like your friends, son.

JOHN PRYNNE I'll choose them.

PRYNNE Gaiety and folly.
    Make a virtue of humility,
    Be Christian.

JOHN PRYNNE Where will that get me?
    Christ was only a bloody Jew, dad.
    Didn't you teach me that?
    When did you get converted?

PRYNNE Be loving.
    All men and women.

JOHN PRYNNE I'm choosy. I hate . . . old women who mention
    their legs . . . and young men with dark hair and
    big noses!
    They hate me, don't they?
    Why should I accept people who live in ignorance
    like . . . like beasts, eh?
    The scum of the earth. I'm proud, father.
    I'm trying to make my way, dad.
    I'm a man. I'm proud, sir!
    I am my father's son!!

PRYNNE Don't talk so loudly.

JOHN PRYNNE I like loving as well. Don't get me wrong.

PRYNNE Be loving. Be Christian.

JOHN PRYNNE (*making kissing sounds*).
    I am, father. I like giving flowers. I'm learning.

PRYNNE You disgust me.

JOHN PRYNNE I like kissing. I like necking. I like petting. You
    name it.

PRYNNE Ugh! Men will use you for their sport,
    Like a horse or a dog.
    O for the seraphic kiss,
    Of purest love,
    Of innocence, of peace.
    No taint, no shame.

    I'm dying.

JOHN PRYNNE So you keep saying.

PRYNNE Keep away from excess, for the sake of all that is
dear and lovely to you in life.

Do not desert your post.

JOHN PRYNNE }
PRYNNE } *(together).*

It is only a matter of will-power!

Enter TERESA, *dolled up, with microscopic skirt.*

PRYNNE I'm dying.

Is it romantic to be dying?

To a woman?

JOHN PRYNNE You're pale.

You're ill.

What is it?

PRYNNE I'm dying.

JOHN PRYNNE What do you mean, dying?

PRYNNE I'm dying, my son.

Smell my breath,

Smell the grave in me.

JOHN PRYNNE Dying? You're dying!

But me?! I've got nothing!!

What is to become of me, dad?!!!

They embrace, JOHN PRYNNE *sobbing.*

(Writhing.) I'm your son, father!

I love you!

TERESA *runs off.*

SCENE FOURTEEN

ROSIE, *blooming, making-up.*

ROSIE Where are you, John Patrick, my lover?

Arthur!

Are you sleeping?
Coo-ee!
He's sleeping.
Thank god I'm gettin' away regular,
From his bleeding whining, this bloody television.
'What about the workers?'
Hee-hee. 'Corse he votes tory.
(*Shouting.*) 'Stuff the bleeding workers!'
(*Singing and
swaying.*) I'm going out tonight,
I'm going on the town tonight.
I'm happy, that's what counts, isn't it my darling,
O my prince charming?

I'm going to a concert. Arthur thinks I'm going to
bingo.
Getting a dose, I am . . . of culture, really.
It's very good for you,
It's so improving,
It makes me feel much better,
Mr Ross likes his music.
Let him have it, I say.
He's so . . . so fun-loving, underneath the surface,
It doesn't do any harm, does it, not really?
It's harmless.
It makes us very romantic,
Nutcracker Suit and that,
So . . . sweeping, isn't it?

I have to think of the future,
Arthur's days are numbered,
I'm hoping for a proposal . . . after,
Rosie Ross, it's very euphonious, that's what John
Patrick says,

Well it is, really,
He's part English, part Irish, part Scottish,
A hopeless mish-mash truly,
Still I'm not complaining,
I'm not really racial.
Knocks at the door.
O my darling,
O my prince charming.
I'm decking out my own sweet body.
De-odorant in armpit.
Freshening up my secret places.
We don't want no unpleasant surprises.
Right then!
Here I come!
I'm sailing.
She goes to, and opens, the door, sinks into ROSS's *arms, at length.*
You naughty man.
You've got me going.
I feel quite tempestuous,
Really torrid already. You're a very fast worker.
It must be the weather.

ROSS Where's Arthur?

ROSIE You're so daring.
He's sleeping.

ROSS I don't feel like going out.

ROSIE O John Patrick!
Really!

ROSS I'm tired.
He puts his face in her capacious bosom.
I want to hide from the hurry of the world.

ROSIE Darling!

ROSS I want to cover my face.
He nuzzles her breasts.
See nothing, save this and this.

Give me kisses, and the breastmilk of love.
I care nothing for life itself. This only.
They sink on to the sofa, nuzzling, ROSS *trying to unfasten her clothes.*

ROSIE Stop it, really!
On our own sofa!
It isn't reasonable.
I'm so happy.
What are you doing?

ROSS The parrot never puts his foot on a twig,
Till he's tried it with his beak, Rosie.

ROSIE Is that what you teach your students?

ROSS I learned it . . . on the bush . . . telegraph.

ROSIE Don't be so vulgar!
Do you love me, darling?

ROSS Love is what a man might term a poetic fancy,
A vice brought to a fine art,
A gross act, made fair in the mind.
That's all.

ROSIE O what beauty! So wordy!

I understand, my lover.
You don't believe in love, do you, John Patrick?

ROSS I can if I wish.
I want to touch you like this, all over.
An orgasm is enough.
That is love.

ROSIE No.

ROSS Please!

ROSIE No!

ROSS It's wrong, it's a crime.

ROSIE I thought there was no such thing, eh, clever?
That's what you told me, you naughty.
Enter ARTHUR, *creeping, muffled, in dressing gown, watching, as they descend again, writhing, embracing.*

> Oh, my darling!
> You're making me so restless, touching me like that.
> I'm getting so heated.
> O, darling!
> What are you doing? Tell me!

ARTHUR (*wheezing*).
> We are the people!

(*Softly.*) Rosie! My lady-wife!
> My darling! I'm Arthur Brackley!
> I'm your hubby!
> I've got coronary thrombosis.

ROSIE (*to* ROSS).
> O my darling lover, I'm swooning!
> Take me!

SCENE FIFTEEN

STRONG, *much older, playing cards with his silent* HOUSEKEEPER.

STRONG (*chuckling*).
> What an abysmal death!
> What a parody of life was Prynne's!
> *Housekeeper chuckles.*

(*Playing a card.*) But death is inevitable even for the ideal man, Miss Lewis.
> Yet the thought of death is bearable,
> For I know that all must die.

In time,

95

          Some of the causes of decay
          Will perhaps be eradicated from the human body . . .
          A silence.

HOUSEKEEPER . . . Snap!

    STRONG When that has been done,
          Then we shall improve our natural state.
          Though we cannot roll back the tide of death . . .
          Snap! . . .
          We can set our faces steadily to life's future.
          It is the sacred and sworn duty of all men,
          To do something to this end.

HOUSEKEEPER Snap!

    STRONG That is my delight and pleasure, Miss Lewis.
          If the eye is always watching,
          And the mind is on the alert,
          Chance will supply the happy occasions for help . . .

HOUSEKEEPER . . . Snap!

    STRONG (*drinking*).
          Men lack awareness, that is all . . .

HOUSEKEEPER . . . Snap!

    STRONG If the graves were opened,
          And the dead began to walk,
          The mass of the people would soon ignore it.
          That is the sublime pathos of human life.
          They both chuckle.
          O tempora!
          O mores!

HOUSEKEEPER Snap!

    STRONG I've had enough.
          Bring me my supper.
          Exit HOUSEKEEPER.
   (*Drinking.*) Aaaah!
          I prefer my own torments.
          Nothing is intolerable that is necessary.
          He lights a cigar.

Prayer can be signified by the hand or the eye,
By a thought or a groan.
No more is needed, no clamour.

It is up to me whether life will end in victory, or
surrender.
Entirely.
The wretched man is merely he who thinks himself
so.

V.S.O.P.
Splendid.

It is in goodness of will that we find our peace.
I have collapsed into benevolence.
I see everything.
All is well.
I am, in myself, myself wholly.
I am full of memories.
I have trodden the wide, well-beaten, tracks of the
world.

All is well.
There is no need for me to do more.
Truth can defend itself.
To Doctor Thomas Strong, bachelor of medicine,
Ladies and gentlemen,
Death does not yet beckon.
He puffs cigar.
Life goes on,
Life goes on,
All is well.
A silence.
As for other men's griefs,
There is no known consolation.

There is no relief,
There is no hope certain
Well, what of it?
(*Looking into
  his glass.*) Only give me life strong and full as the brimming
ocean,
(*Standing up,
  swaying.*) And I shall stand up for ever.
My life is my prayer.

If others wish to fill their hearts with bubbles,
So be it.

I grieve for wrong, but suffer . . . no pain.
There is no need for me to do any more!
Life goes on, death does not yet beckon,
All is well,
I am Thomas Strong,
Life goes on, all is well.
Enter HOUSEKEEPER *with tray of steaming food, as in
Scene One.*
(*Taking tray.*) I am Thomas Strong, I am Thomas Strong!
HOUSEKEEPER Yes, sir.
That's it, sir.

Methuen's Modern Plays

EDITED BY JOHN CULLEN

★   ★   ★

Methuen's Theatre Classics

★   ★   ★

Methuen Playscripts